in times of

grieving

Praise for *In Times of Grieving*

This book offers a chorus of voices in prayer that know the pain of grieving and yet chant the music of God's healing. The many prayers herein, some ancient . . . some new, are sensitive and soothing, yet they go beyond comforting, they offer nothing short of transformation.

—**Richard P. Johnson, Ph.D.**
Association for Lifelong Adult Ministry

Praise for the *In Times of . . .* series

Life has hard times and the hardest sometimes is when we have to help ourselves or others through hard times. Where are we to get the insight, the resources to encourage and strengthen us? Where can we find the biblical passages to read and meditate by ourselves or with others? How can we express ourselves in faith when we are fearful, angry, exhausted or doubtful?

Robert Hamma has the answer. In three brief, helpful books of ten sections each he gives us psalms, canticles, gospel passages, and his own meditations that comfort, cheer and inspire us in time of need.

—**William G. Storey, D.M.S.**
Author of *Lord Hear Our Prayer*

A simple, consoling collection of prayers for those who are sick, grieving, or giving care to others. It will be a wonderful help for people in times of stress and distress, particularly helping them to pray in and through their real lives and intense emotions. I recommend it as a healing resource for every Christian community.

—**Fr. Stephen Rossetti**
St. Luke Institute

PRAYERS OF COMFORT & CONSOLATION

in times of

grieving

Robert M. Hamma

ave maria press AmP Notre Dame, Indiana

---

www.avemariapress.com

International Standard Book Number: 1-59471-016-3

Cover and text design by John Carson

Printed and bound in the United States of America.

Library of Congress Cataloging-in-Publication Data
Hamma, Robert M.
  In times of grieving : prayers of comfort and consolation / Robert M. Hamma.
      p. cm.
  Includes index.
  ISBN 1-59471-016-3 (pbk.)
1. Bereavement--Religious aspects--Christianity. 2. Grief--Religious aspects--Christianity. 3. Death--Religious aspects--Christianity.
4. Consolation. I. Title.

  BV4905.3.H36 2004
  242'.866--dc22

                              2004006155

Contents

Introduction ... 7

Everyday Prayers ... 13

1 / When You Are in Shock ... 20

2 / When You Are Angry ... 30

3 / When You Are Afraid ... 39

4 / When You Are Overwhelmed ... 49

5 / When Your Faith Is Weak ... 58

6 / When You Are Feeling Hopeless ... 68

7 / When You Want to Accept Your Loss ... 77

8 / When You Want to Pray for the Deceased ... 87

9 / When You Are Grateful ... 98

10 / When You Want to Remember ... 110

Index of Prayers ... 119

Acknowledgments ... 121

Introduction

We are never really ready to cope with the death of someone we love.

Whether the death follows a long and debilitating illness, or comes suddenly, unexpectedly, it releases a flood of emotions. Perhaps you have been holding these emotions back until now, putting all your energy into caring for your loved one during an illness. Perhaps, if this death was totally unexpected, you are in a state of shock, struggling to come to terms with this loss, to accept that the unthinkable has happened. Or perhaps you have been buoyed for a time by an outpouring of love and support through the wake and the funeral, but now find yourself alone, beset by thoughts and feelings that seem too much to handle.

Each of us grieves differently, in our own way. There is no schedule, no timetable to tell us how long it will take. And we don't necessarily make progress every day. We may be stuck for awhile, feeling like it will never end. We may have hard days when we least expect them; we may have easy days when we think we shouldn't. Grief is not manageable. It is not a problem to be solved or a disease to be cured. It is a long and difficult journey.

We never get over our loss, but somehow we learn to live with it. Perhaps one day we will discover that we have even grown from it. As the writer Gerald Sittser said in his book *A Grace Disguised*, "Sorrow took up permanent residence in my soul and enlarged it."

We make this journey of grief alone, in the company of our thoughts and feelings. We make it with others who share our grief and care for us. And we make it with God, who is always with us. So let us be gentle with ourselves and avoid placing expectations on our grieving. But at the same time, let us not run from our grief, steeling ourselves against the pain.

The journey of grief will give rise to emotions that may be unfamiliar, perhaps uncomfortable. They may be feelings of fear, despair, anger, guilt, or even relief. If we acknowledge our feelings and name them for what they are, we bring them from the dark hidden recesses of our hearts and into the light of day where they can be accepted and healed.

The journey of grief will call us to be vulnerable, to allow others into the private and deeply personal places in our hearts. We may struggle with our tears, knowing that they reveal our neediness, our inability to go through this alone. But we are not alone in our grieving. Other family members and friends share our sorrow, each in their own way. And remember that the depth of the loss that you feel is an expression of the depth of the love you shared with the one who died. That deep capacity to give and receive love is a lasting legacy of your beloved, and it is still within you.

The third dimension of our lives that the journey of grief calls forth is our dependence on God. God's comfort and healing come to us in very personal ways. God is present as we make this journey and subtly speaks to us through our feelings, even those feelings that may be most difficult to accept. God is present through our family and friends and can touch us and console us through their hands and their words. But God is greater than the confines of our hearts or the capacity of our loved ones to care for us. Jesus, the Good Shepherd, searches for us, his lost sheep, never ceasing to seek us out and carry us safely home.

Prayer is like a compass on this journey, keeping us on the path, showing us the way. When we pray, we open ourselves more widely to receive God's love and care. When we pray we are more able to recognize that God is indeed with us, walking alongside us on this long and difficult journey.

Using This Book

This book is written simply to help you pray. While it has a certain structure and format, feel free to use it as you wish. Hopefully the format of psalms, scripture, prayers, and meditations will make it easy and flexible to use.

In Times Of Grieving is organized into ten chapters. Each of these chapters focuses on particular feelings that we often experience during grief. These emotions, whether positive, such as trust or gratitude, or negative, such as loneliness or fear, can be very helpful starting points for prayer. If prayer is an expression of the heart, then the feelings in our hearts are a good place to begin. A brief introduction to each chapter helps bring the dimensions of each experience to the surface and invites us to turn to God in the midst of those experiences.

Within each of these chapters, there are two sections. The first is called "A Brief Time of Prayer." The structure of this part is as follows:

> Psalm
> Reading
> Breath Prayer
> Closing Prayer

A psalm has been chosen that expresses the particular feeling or disposition within us at this particular moment. A brief line, traditionally called an antiphon, expresses the theme of the psalm and is normally recited before and after the psalm is prayed. Then a "psalm prayer" reiterates the theme of the psalm in light of the experience of grieving. Next, a brief gospel reading speaks to us about what we are going through. It helps us identify with a moment in the life of Jesus or one of his followers when they too experienced something like what we are experiencing here and now.

A brief time of reflection after the reading is helpful if one is able, otherwise move directly to the next part, a one-line prayer called a "breath prayer." This prayer is modeled on the ancient practice of the Jesus Prayer, which is repeated meditatively in rhythm with one's breathing: "Lord Jesus Christ, Son of the living God, have mercy on me, a sinner." The breath prayers in each chapter can also be easily prayed with the rhythm of our breathing. For example, the breath prayer during times when you are afraid is, "Fear not, for I am with you." The first phrase, "Fear not," can be spoken inwardly as you breathe in, and the second, "for I am with you," can be prayed as you breathe out. This process can be repeated for as long as you wish. Indeed, it can be used throughout the day or in the lonely hours of the night.

The brief time of prayer ends with a closing prayer, either the Lord's Prayer or one of the biblical canticles found in the Everyday Prayers section of the book. While the brief time of prayer can be used at any time of day, the concluding canticles are taken from the church's morning, evening, and night prayer and may be selected accordingly.

Each brief time of prayer can be prayed alone or with another. Indeed, one way that this book can be best used is as a prayer resource for family members, friends, or a grief group to use together. The prayers and readings in the second part of each chapter may also be used in the context of these brief times of prayer.

The second section of each chapter offers prayers and readings that can be used as the need arises. The prayers are taken from a variety of classic and contemporary sources. Those not attributed to another source have been composed by the author. There are two additional readings, one from scripture and another from a spiritual writer whose reflections offer insight and consolation during these times.

Prayer reminds us that we are not alone as we go through hard times. Whether our loved ones are present to offer us comfort and support, or at a distance, prayer reminds us of their love and concern. Likewise, the words of the psalms, prayers, and readings place us in touch with Christians throughout the world and with previous generations who have used these very words to find courage and strength in times of need. And these prayers remind us that the Lord, our shepherd and our friend, is with us always.

Everyday Prayers

Morning Prayer

My God, I give you this day.
I offer you now
all the good that I shall do,
and I thank you now
for the joys that it may bring.
I will try to accept, for the sake of your love,
whatever difficulties or setbacks I may
  experience.
Help me to live this day in your consoling
  presence
and to conduct myself in a way that pleases you.
  —Based on a prayer by St. Francis de Sales

Evening Prayer

My dearest Lord,
as this day ends and evening comes,
I place myself again in your consoling hands.
Be thou a bright flame before me,
a guiding star above me,
a smooth path beneath me,
a kindly shepherd behind me, today, tonight,
  and forever.
  —Based on a prayer by St. Columba

Night Prayer

Save us Lord while we are awake,
and guard us as we sleep,
that awake we may watch with Christ,
and asleep, rest in his peace.

And may the souls of the faithful departed,
through the mercy of God
rest in peace. Amen.
  —Office of Compline, Roman Breviary

Canticle of Zachary

This biblical song is traditionally prayed as part of the church's morning prayer.

Blessed be the Lord, the God of Israel;
he has come to his people and set them free.
He has raised up for us a mighty Savior,
born of the house of his servant David.

Through his holy prophets he promised of old
that he would save us from our enemies,
from the hands of all who hate us.
He promised to show mercy to our ancestors
and to remember his holy covenant.

This was the oath he swore to our father
Abraham:
to set us free from the hands of our enemies,
free to worship him without fear,
holy and righteous in his sight
all the days of our life.

You, my child, shall be called the prophet of the
Most High;
for you will go before the Lord to prepare his
way,

to give his people knowledge of salvation
by the forgiveness of their sins.

In the tender compassion of our God
the dawn from on high shall break upon us,
to shine on those who dwell in darkness and the
    shadow of death,
and to guide our feet on the way to peace.

Glory be to the Father, and to the Son
    and to the Holy Spirit:
as it was in the beginning, is now,
    and will be forever. Amen.

Canticle of Mary

This biblical song is traditionally prayed as part of the church's evening prayer.

My soul proclaims the greatness of the Lord,
my spirit rejoices in God, my Savior;
for he has looked with favor on his lowly servant.

From this day all generations will call me blessed:
for the Almighty has done great things for me,
and holy is his Name.

He has mercy on those who fear him
in every generation.

He has shown the strength of his arm,
he has scattered the proud in their conceit.

He has cast down the mighty from their thrones,
and has lifted up the lowly.

He has filled the hungry with good things,
and the rich he has sent away empty.

He has come to the help of his servant Israel
for he has remembered his promise of mercy,
the promise he made to our ancestors,
to Abraham and his children forever.

Glory be to the Father, and to the Son
    and to the Holy Spirit:
as it was in the beginning, is now,
    and will be forever. Amen.

Canticle of Simeon

This biblical song is traditionally prayed as part of the church's night prayer.

Lord, now let your servant go in peace;
your word has been fulfilled:

my own eyes have seen the salvation
which you have prepared in the sight
    of every people;
a light to reveal you to the nations
and the glory of your people Israel.

Glory be to the Father, and to the Son
    and to the Holy Spirit:
as it was in the beginning, is now,
    and will be forever. Amen.

Chapter 1

When You Are In Shock

In the hours and days after the loss of a loved one, nothing seems real. Many people feel like they are living in a nightmare from which there is no escape. Our emotions swirl—from horror, to disbelief, to numbness. Our hearts are broken and our minds are blank.

When we experience such terrifying feelings we are terribly helpless. The feelings are beyond our control and there is nothing we can do. We may sob or scream, we may pound our fists or break something. Whatever we do, it is alright. We have to express these emotions.

But at the same time there is a poor, helpless child within us who needs to be held and comforted, sheltered and protected. Let that voice be heard, too. Let those who love you comfort you. If they are wise, they will not give you explanations. They will simply hold you. Let them.

Do not be afraid to bring all these conflicting feelings to God. For Jesus too experienced the shock of loss and understands the pain, the anger, the questions in your heart. Perhaps someone can pray with you, using these simple prayers as a guide.

❧ A Brief Time of Prayer ❧

Psalm 130:1–2, 5–8

Antiphon: I cry to you, O Lord.

Out of the depths I cry to you, O LORD.
Lord, hear my voice!
Let your ears be attentive
to the voice of my supplications!

I wait for the LORD, my soul waits,
and in his word I hope;
my soul waits for the Lord
more than those who watch for the morning,
more than those who watch for the morning.
O Israel, hope in the LORD!
For with the LORD there is steadfast love,
and with him is great power to redeem.
It is he who will redeem Israel from all its
    iniquities.

Repeat Antiphon

Psalm Prayer

Lord, in the midst of this darkness I turn to you. I have nowhere else to go; without you I will be truly lost. My soul waits for you, my spirit clings to you. Throughout my life, you have never left me alone. Be near to me now.

Reading

Luke 23:44–46, 23:50, 23:52–53, 24:1–7
If we die with the Lord, we too shall live with him.

It was now about noon, and darkness came over the whole land until three in the afternoon, while the sun's light failed; and the curtain of the temple was torn in two. Then Jesus, crying with a loud voice, said, "Father, into your hands I commend my spirit." Having said this, he breathed his last.

Now there was a good and righteous man named Joseph, who, though a member of the council. . . . This man went to Pilate and asked for the body of Jesus. Then he took it down, wrapped it in a linen cloth, and laid it in a rock-hewn tomb where no one had ever been laid.

But on the first day of the week, at early dawn, they came to the tomb, taking the spices that they had prepared. They found the stone rolled away from the tomb, but when they went in, they did not find the body. While they were perplexed about this, suddenly two men in dazzling clothes stood beside them. The women were terrified and bowed their faces to the ground, but the men said to them, "Why do you look for the living among the dead? He is not here, but has risen. Remember how he told you, while he was still in Galilee, that the Son of Man must be handed over to sinners, and be crucified, and on the third day rise again."

Breath Prayer

Repeat this prayer in rhythm with your breathing for as long as you wish.

My life is in your hands.

Closing Prayer

Pray the Our Father or one of the Canticles in the Everyday Prayers section of the book.

❦ Prayers In Times of Shock ❧

Experiencing Loss

All-Embracing Love,
your circle of strength
is around me.

I ask for grace to yield
to the reality of this loss.
I pray to surrender
to what cannot be changed.
I beg for deliverance
from the emotional drain
and the unending sadness
that this loss has brought me.

Let peace return.
Let hope begin.
Let comfort be mine.
   —Joyce Rupp

The Torn Curtain

"Darkness came over the whole land . . .
the sun's light failed;
and the curtain of the temple was torn in two . . ."
at the hour of your death, O Lord.

Now, at this hour of death, O Lord,
darkness covers my world,
the light of my life has failed,
and the fabric of my heart is torn asunder.

Ripped, shredded, beyond mending.
Good for nothing, or so it seems.
Take this darkness, this black hole of grief,
this shredded life.

I don't know what else to do,
but to cry out to you
for light, for hope, for comfort.

Stabat Mater

At the cross her station keeping,
Mary stood in sorrow weeping,
  When her son was crucified.

While she waited in her anguish,
Seeing Christ in torment languish,
  Bitter sorrow pierced her heart.

With what pain and desolation,
With what noble resignation,
  Mary watched her dying Son.

Ever patient in her yearning,
Though her tear filled eyes were burning,
  Mary gazed upon her Son.

Who, that sorrow contemplating,
On that passion meditating,
  Would not share the Virgin's grief?

Christ she saw for our salvation,
Scourged with cruel acclamation,
  Bruised and beaten by the rod.

Christ she saw with life-blood failing,
All her anguish unavailing,
  Saw him breathe his very last.

Mary fount of love's devotion,
Let me share with true emotion,
  all the sorrows you endured.

Mary, mother of all sorrows, I turn to you in my
grief. You who know the pain I feel, enfold me in
your compassion, and lead me to the healing
mercy of your Son Jesus, crucified, yet risen.
  —Jacopone da Todi, trans. by Anthony G. Petti

O Living God

Ah Lord, my prayers are dead,
my affections are dead,
and my heart is dead;
But you are a living God,
and I commit myself to you.
  —William Bridge

❧ Readings for Times of Shock ❧

Acknowledge Your Pain *Tears are often a necessary way to allow ourselves to feel the pain within us.*

Let your tears flow when you feel them welling within you. It is a blessed and sacred release. Tears are cleansing and healing. Like a sudden summer rain shower, when the sun peaks through once again after the cloudburst, so will you feel at peace after a good crying spell. Visualize your tears washing away the dark stain of sorrow on your soul. Cry for all that you have loved and lost, give yourself over to your grieving and let it expend itself. It is the suppression of grief that causes a festering in your soul. Acknowledge your pain, give it to God, and let it go.

—Ann Dawson

Lamentations 3:17–26 *In the midst of our shock and disbelief at what has befallen us, we struggle to hold on as we await God's help.*

My soul is bereft of peace; I have forgotten what happiness is; so I say, "Gone is my glory, and all that I had hoped for from the Lord." The thought of my affliction and my homelessness is wormwood and gall! My soul continually thinks of it and is bowed down within me.

But this I call to mind, and therefore I have hope: The steadfast love of the LORD never ceases, his mercies never come to an end; they are new every morning; great is your faithfulness. "The LORD is my portion," says my soul, "therefore I will hope in him." The LORD is good to those who wait for him, to the soul that seeks him. It is good that one should wait quietly for the salvation of the LORD.

Chapter 2

When You Are Angry

Anger is a natural and normal response to the loss of a loved one. The closeness of our relationship and the circumstances of death can affect the depth and the length of our anger. For some, anger is easily recognized and readily expressed. For others, anger is a difficult emotion to name, and it takes time to recognize it. Either way, we need to come to terms with our anger and recognize why we feel the way we do. We may be angry with people who were involved with our loved one at the time of death, such as doctors or nurses. Or we may be angry with our loved one who died, thinking perhaps that this death could have been avoided. We may also be angry with God. Acknowledging our anger is the first step toward healing and peace.

Bringing this difficult emotion to prayer can help us take a step back from our struggle. It's okay to express our anger toward God. There's a long tradition in the Bible of faithful people who let God know just how angry they were. Remembering that Jesus got angry sometimes, at his disciples as well as his adversaries, can give us some added perspective on this confusing emotion.

❦ A Brief Time of Prayer ❧

Psalm 55:1–8, 17–18

Antiphon: Do not hide from me, O Lord.

Give ear to my prayer, O God;
do not hide yourself from my supplication.
Attend to me, and answer me;
I am troubled in my complaint.
I am distraught by the noise of the enemy,
because of the clamor of the wicked.
For they bring trouble upon me,
 and in anger they cherish enmity against me.

My heart is in anguish within me,
the terrors of death have fallen upon me.
Fear and trembling come upon me,
and horror overwhelms me.
And I say, "O that I had wings like a dove!
I would fly away and be at rest;
truly, I would flee far away;
I would lodge in the wilderness;
I would hurry to find a shelter for myself
 from the raging wind and tempest."

Evening and morning and at noon
I utter my complaint and moan, and he will hear
my voice.
He will redeem me unharmed from the battle
that I wage,
for many are arrayed against me.

Repeat Antiphon

Psalm Prayer

All day long and all through the night I cry out to
you, O Lord. I rock with grief, I groan in anger.
Do not abandon me, but hear me and give me
comfort. Teach me again how to trust in you.

Reading

Mark 15:33–34 *We cry out with Jesus.*

When it was noon, darkness came over the whole
land until three in the afternoon. At three o'clock
Jesus cried out with a loud voice, "Eloi, Eloi, lema
sabachthani?" which means, "My God, my god,
why have you forsaken me?"

Breath Prayer

Repeat this prayer in rhythm with your breathing for as long as you wish.

Your love, O Lord, is stronger than death.

Closing Prayer

Pray the Our Father or one of the Canticles in the Everyday Prayers section of the book.

❧ Prayers for Coping With Anger ❦

Just Be Here, Lord

Sometimes I hate you, God! There, I've said it, and now you know how angry I am, how furious I feel that you would do this to me.

But I guess you knew that already since you know everything, since you know me so well. People tell me this anger will pass, that I'll be OK. I don't want to hear it. So please, don't say anything Lord. Just be here, OK? And let me blow off some steam and maybe I'll feel better . . . though I doubt it.

You're the only one who's not afraid of my anger, who can take it all and still love me. So just be here, OK?

Were You Angry Too, Jesus?

Jesus, were you angry when your prayer was not heard, when the cup would not pass, when you cried out, "Why have you abandoned me?" I know you got angry at the Pharisees and at the money changers. It would help to think that you might have, for one little minute, been angry with your Father. If you could be that angry, then I guess I could too.

I don't like being angry, but I am. And I can't make it go away, as much as I may want to. Could you just be with me in this anger, in this pain, in this emptiness? I don't know what I'll do if you're not.

Why God?

Why God? Why now?

There was so much to live for,
so much ahead of us, so many dreams.
Now they are all gone.

Do you hear me, God?
Do you know how angry I am?
My heart is broken, my hands are bleeding.

My anger is a sharp-edged stone,
but I am clutching it tightly,
it's all I have right now.

Will you give me something else to hold on to?

When Anger Imprisons You

O Lord my God, I have hope in thee;
O my dear Jesus, set me free.
Though hard the chains that fasten me
and sore my lot, yet I long for thee.
I languish and groaning bend my knee,
adoring, imploring, O set me free.
   —Mary, Queen of Scots

Anger Is Often Difficult *Only if we allow ourselves to experience anger can we find a way through it.*

Souls who walk in light sing the hymns of light; those who walk in the shadows chant the hymns of darkness. Each must be allowed to sing through to the end the words and melody which God has given him. Nothing must be changed in what God composed. Every drop of distress, bitter as gall though it may be, must be allowed to flow, no matter what its effect on us. It was the same for Jeremiah and Ezekiel, whose every utterance was broken by sighs and tears. They found consolation only by continuing their laments. Had their tears been halted, we should have lost the loveliest passages in Scripture. The spirit which makes us suffer is the only one which can comfort us. These different waters flow from the same source. . . . We [must] let the divine project develop, for within itself it contains both the disease and the cure.

—Jean-Pierre de Caussade

Luke 23:32, 39–43 *While anger is a natural response to loss, even in the midst of anger, we may choose to trust.*

Two others also, who were criminals, were led away to be put to death with him. One of the criminals who were hanged there kept deriding him and saying, "Are you not the Messiah? Save yourself and us!" But the other rebuked him, saying, "Do you not fear God, since you are under the same sentence of condemnation? And we indeed have been condemned justly, for we are getting what we deserve for our deeds, but this man has done nothing wrong." Then he said, "Jesus, remember me when you come into your kingdom." He replied, "Truly I tell you, today you will be with me in Paradise."

Chapter 3

When You Are Afraid

"No one ever told me that grief feels so like fear," C. S. Lewis once wrote. We lose so much when a loved one dies—the intimacy, the friendship, the sense of purpose, the awareness that we are known and loved. We feel alone, and so naturally we feel afraid.

We may want to hide, to shut out the world and protect ourselves. Fear can certainly have a paralyzing effect on us. But at the same time we may feel an impulse to turn to others for strength and support. Yet this can seem so difficult, so frightening.

As we struggle to find the courage to be vulnerable in the midst of our fears, perhaps we can remember that there are many people who love and care for us. They may indeed want to help, but just don't know how. Perhaps we can open ourselves to them in some small way at first and learn to trust little by little.

Let these prayers help you open your heart not only to others but to God who seeks to surround you with his loving kindness.

❧ A Brief Time of Prayer ❧

Psalm 27:1–5, 7–11, 13

Antiphon: Let your heart take courage in the Lord.

The LORD is my light and my salvation;
whom shall I fear?
The LORD is the stronghold of my life;
of whom shall I be afraid?
When evildoers assail me to devour my flesh—
   my adversaries and foes—they shall stumble
   and fall.

Though an army encamp against me,
my heart shall not fear;
though war rise up against me,
yet I will be confident.
One thing I asked of the LORD,
that will I seek after:
to live in the house of the LORD
all the days of my life,
to behold the beauty of the Lord,
   and to inquire in his temple.

For he will hide me in his shelter in the day
 of trouble;
he will conceal me under the cover of his tent;
he will set me high on a rock. . . .

Hear, O Lord, when I cry aloud,
be gracious to me and answer me!
"Come," my heart says, "seek his face!"
Your face, Lord, do I seek.
Do not hide your face from me.
Do not turn your servant away in anger,
you who have been my help.
Do not cast me off, do not forsake me,
O God of my salvation!

If my father and mother forsake me,
the Lord will take me up.
Teach me your way, O Lord,
and lead me on a level path. . . .
I believe that I shall see the goodness of the Lord
in the land of the living.
Wait for the Lord; be strong,
and let your heart take courage;
wait for the Lord!

Repeat Antiphon

Psalm Prayer

Lord, you know the fear in my heart, the uncertainty, the worry. As much as I want to let go of it, to be free, I don't know how. Help me to trust in your presence, in your guidance and protection. As long as you are with me, I am never alone.

Reading

John 14:1–7 *Like Jesus' disciple, we are afraid because we do not know the way.*

"Do not let your hearts be troubled. Believe in God, believe also in me. In my Father's house there are many dwelling places. If it were not so, would I have told you that I go to prepare a place for you? And if I go and prepare a place for you, I will come again and will take you to myself, so that where I am, there you may be also. And you know the way to the place where I am going." Thomas said to him, "Lord, we do not know where you are going. How can we know the way?" Jesus said to him, "I am the way, and the truth, and the life. No one comes to the Father except through me. If you know me, you will know my Father also. From now on you do know him and have seen him."

Breath Prayer

Repeat this prayer in rhythm with your breathing for as long as you wish.

Fear not, for I am with you.

Closing Prayer

Pray the Our Father or one of the Canticles in the Everyday Prayers section of the book.

❧ Prayers for Coping With Fear ☙

I Am Afraid

Lord, I am afraid.
I feel lost, abandoned, alone.
I want to shut out the world,
to hide away in some safe place.
But there is nowhere to go
that this fear does not follow.
When I try to summon up my courage,
there is nothing there.
Only this impulse to hide.
"Perfect love casts out fear," you said.
Only your love is perfect, Lord,
mine is weak and fragile.
Open my heart to receive your love.
Touch me gently, carefully, with your comfort.
Help me to allow others to console me,
by their words, their presence, their touch.
Let your perfect love cast this fear out of
    my heart.

Lead, Kindly Light

Lead, kindly Light, amid the encircling gloom,
    lead Thou me on!
The night is dark, and I am far from home—
    lead Thou me on!
Keep Thou my feet; I do not ask to see
The distant scene—one step enough for me.
I was not ever thus, nor pray'd that Thou
    shouldst lead me on.
I loved to choose and see my path, but now
    lead Thou me on!
I loved the garish day, and, spit of fears,
Pride ruled my will: remember not past years.
So long Thy power hath blest me, sure it still
    will lead me on,
o'er moor and fen, o'er crag and torrent, till
    the night is gone;
and with the morn those angel faces smile
which I have loved long since, and last awhile.
    —John Henry Newman

Be Within Me Lord

Be Lord, within me to strengthen me,
without me to preserve me,
over me to shelter me,
beneath me to support me,
before me to divert me,
behind me to bring me back,
and round about me to fortify me.
 —Lancelot Andrewes

❧ Readings for Times of Fear ❧

Putting Fear Into Perspective *While fear may seem crippling, we are not helpless.*

Did you ever notice how much scarier some problem seems when you wake up thinking about it in the middle of the night? Fear thrives in the dark, which is why the first step in getting a handle on your fears is to bring them out in the open and look at them straight on.

"The worst fear is a hidden fear, the nagging fear at the back of your mind," says David Rensberger, Ph.D., a professor of New Testament studies at the Interdenominational Theological Center in Atlanta. "The way to deal with that is to lead it out in the center of your mind and get to know it. That allows you to put your fears in context. Often when you do that the fear shrinks—it doesn't seem so overwhelming."

Here are two steps that can cut what's scaring you down to size.

1. Write them down: "Get your fears out of your heart and head and put them onto paper," suggests the Rev. Corrin Morris, an Episcopal priest who directs the Interweave Center for Holistic Living in Summit, New Jersey. This helps you decide which fears are real and which may be figments of your imagination.

2. Know your enemy: If it is true that what scares us the most is the unknown, then it stands to reason that knowing more will help you fear less. So, if you find a fear overwhelming, research it thoroughly and see if this helps shrink fears to a more manageable size.
—Doug Hill

Isaiah 43:1–5 *In the midst of our many real fears, perhaps our greatest source of comfort is recalling that we are loved deeply and personally by God.*

But now thus says the LORD, he who created you, O Jacob, he who formed you, O Israel: Do not fear, for I have redeemed you; I have called you by name, you are mine. When you pass through the waters, I will be with you; and through the rivers, they shall not overwhelm you; when you walk through fire you shall not be burned, and the flame shall not consume you. For I am the LORD your God, the Holy One of Israel, your Savior. I give Egypt as your ransom, Ethiopia and Seba in exchange for you. Because you are precious in my sight, and honored, and I love you, I give people in return for you, nations in exchange for your life. Do not fear, for I am with you; I will bring your offspring from the east, and from the west I will gather you. . . .

Chapter 4

When You Are Overwhelmed

Grieving can sometimes overwhelm us. We may feel listless or depressed, burdened by life's daily responsibilities, exhausted by the simplest task. We may be tired but unable to sleep or sleep all day without refreshment.

Life can be overwhelming in the best of circumstances, so we shouldn't be too surprised when the burden of our grief makes life seem crushing. Loss wounds us deeply, and recovery takes time. We shouldn't expect to have our normal strength. Grief is hard work, and it has no timetable.

We often think of prayer as a source of strength, and indeed God desires to give us the strength we need to recover. But the strength we seek rarely comes as some infusion of divine power in us. Rather, God tends to restore us gradually, healing us day by day. Prayer is a way of resting in God and allowing the Spirit of God to renew us from the inside out.

❧ A Brief Time of Prayer ❧

Psalm 69:1–3, 13–18

Antiphon: In your mercy, Lord, hear my prayer.

Save me, O God, for the waters have come up to
    my neck.
I sink in deep mire, where there is no foothold;
I have come into deep waters, and the flood
    sweeps over me.
I am weary with my crying; my throat is parched.
My eyes grow dim with waiting for my God.

But as for me, my prayer is to you, O LORD.
At an acceptable time, O God,
in the abundance of your steadfast love,
    answer me.
With your faithful help rescue me from sinking in
    the mire;
let me be delivered from my enemies and from
    the deep waters.

Do not let the flood sweep over me,
or the deep swallow me up,
or the Pit close its mouth over me.
Answer me, O LORD, for your steadfast love
  is good;
according to your abundant mercy, turn to me.

Do not hide your face from your servant,
for I am in distress—make haste to answer me.
Draw near to me, redeem me,
set me free because of my enemies.

Repeat Antiphon

Psalm Prayer

I cry to you, O God, for my grief is like a flood
that sweeps me away, like a deep pit that
swallows me. In your mercy, hear my prayer, for I
am in distress. In your abundant love hasten to
help me, for I am overwhelmed. Draw near to
me, O Lord, and rescue me.

Reading

Matthew 11:28–30 *Although we feel overwhelmed, we are not alone.*

"Come to me, all you that are weary and are carrying heavy burdens, and I will give you rest. Take my yoke upon you, and learn from me; for I am gentle and humble in heart, and you will find rest for your souls. For my yoke is easy, and my burden is light."

Breath Prayer

Repeat this prayer in rhythm with your breathing for as long as you wish.

Come to me.

Closing Prayer

Pray the Our Father or one of the Canticles in the Everyday Prayers section of the book.

❧ Prayers When You Are Overwhelmed ❧

For Strength In Weakness

Grant us, Lord, to know in weakness
your strength:
in pain the triumph of your passion,
in poverty the riches of your divinity,
in reproach the satisfaction of your sympathy,
in loneliness the comfort of your continual
presence,
in difficulty the consolation of your intercession,
in confusion the guidance of your wisdom,
and by your glorious death and resurrection
bring us at last to the joy of seeing you
face to face.
  —Author Unknown

O Good Shepherd

O good Shepherd, do not stop searching for me!
For I am exhausted and can't find my way,
lift me up and carry me home to your fold.

O good Samaritan, stop and help me,
for I have been robbed and beaten by death,
carry me to the inn of your mercy.

O good friend, stay by my side,
for I am lonely and disconsolate,
lift this weight from my shoulders
and bear me up.

Weak and Weary

I come to you, O Lord,
weak and weary, heavily burdened.
O gentle, humble Jesus,
teach me how to walk with you
sharing this yoke,
lightening this load.
Give me rest,
give me the peace and consolation
that only you can give.

I Heard the Voice of Jesus Say

I heard the voice of Jesus say, Come unto me and
rest;
Lay down, thou weary one, lay down thy head
upon my breast.
I came to Jesus as I was, weary and worn and sad;
I found in him a resting place, and he has made
me glad.
I heard the voice of Jesus say, Behold, I freely give
The living water; thirsty one, stoop down, and
drink, and live.
I came to Jesus, and I drank of that life-giving
stream;
My thirst was quenched, my soul revived, and
now I live in him.

I heard the voice of Jesus say, I am this dark
world's Light;
Look unto me, thy morn shall rise, and all thy
day be bright.
I looked to Jesus, and I found in him my Star, my
Sun;
And in that light of life I'll walk, till traveling
days are done.

    —Horatius Bonar

❧ Readings When You Are Overwhelmed ❧

Patient Endurance *Sometimes all we can do is hold on.*

It may be that at times the pious and even deeply spiritual literature of the church is too much for average sinners such as you and me. We read of the saints embracing their sufferings with joy and eagerness because their faith assures them of the salvific power of their pains when joined to the sufferings of Christ.

Joy and eagerness are not words that most of us can associate with our crosses. Probably patient endurance is as close as we can get. There are times when we border on or even give in to despair. We call on God in our pain and there is no answer. We seek light at the end of our tunnels and there is only darkness. Even though it offers little consolation, our faith tells us that at no time in our life are we more closely connected to Jesus than when he cried out, "My God, why have you forsaken me?" If we were, at this moment, visited with consolations, our crosses would not be real. We can only cry out with Job, "Even if he slay me, yet I will trust in him." There will be times when we have gone through the dark tunnel and emerged into the light that we are given to realize that God was with us in the darkness, but we could not experience him. There will also be a time when the cross will lead to our physical death and our emergence into the light that will be our resurrection.

—St. Francis de Sales

John 10:11, 14–15, 27–30 *When we feel overwhelmed by all we are carrying, we turn to Jesus, our strong and faithful shepherd.*

"I am the good shepherd. The good shepherd lays down his life for the sheep. . . . I am the good shepherd. I know my own and my own know me, just as the Father knows me and I know the Father. And I lay down my life for the sheep.

"My sheep hear my voice. I know them, and they follow me. I give them eternal life, and they will never perish. No one will snatch them out of my hand. What my Father has given me is greater than all else, and no one can snatch it out of the Father's hand. The Father and I are one."

Chapter 5

When Your Faith Is Weak

We sometimes think that if we have faith, we won't feel the deep sense of sadness for our loss. Or we may think that if we have faith we won't feel like God is absent. We won't feel confused, uncertain, or all alone. So when we find ourselves deep in sadness or doubt, we feel a little guilty, as if it were due to some weakness or failing on our part.

We forget that Jesus wept at his friend Lazarus's death. We forget that Jesus cried to God while on the cross, "Why have you abandoned me?" We forget that faith doesn't exempt us from the pain and struggle of life. Rather, faith calls us to be open to all of life and to receive it as best we can. Faith is not a feeling; it is conviction that God exists and that God loves us. Faith is the belief that despite the darkness that surrounds us, there is a reason to hope for a new day.

Faith is a gift from God, but it is nevertheless a struggle at times. It can be a source of comfort to us to remember that all of Jesus' followers, indeed Jesus himself, had to learn how to grow in faith. And so do we.

❧ A Brief Time of Prayer ❧

Psalm 71:1–3, 5-6, 14–23

Antiphon: Be not far from me; O my God, make haste to help me!

In you, O LORD, I take refuge; let me never be put
    to shame.
In your righteousness deliver me and rescue me;
incline your ear to me and save me.
Be to me a rock of refuge, a strong fortress, to
    save me,
for you are my rock and my fortress.

For you, O LORD, are my hope,
my trust, O LORD, from my youth.
Upon you I have leaned from my birth;
it was you who took me from my mother's womb.
My praise is continually of you.

But I will hope continually, and will praise you
    yet more and more.
My mouth will tell of your righteous acts,
of your deeds of salvation all day long,
though their number is past my knowledge.
I will come praising the mighty deeds of the LORD God,
I will praise your righteousness, yours alone.

O God, from my youth you have taught me,
and I still proclaim your wondrous deeds.
So even to old age and gray hairs, O God, do not
  forsake me,
until I proclaim your might to all the generations
  to come.
Your power and your righteousness, O God,
  reach the high heavens.
You who have done great things, O God, who is
  like you?

You who have made me see many troubles and
  calamities will revive me again;
from the depths of the earth you will
  bring me up again.
You will increase my honor, and comfort me
  once again.
I will also praise you with the harp for your
  faithfulness, O my God;
I will sing praises to you with the lyre,
  O Holy One of Israel.
My lips will shout for joy when I sing praises
  to you;
my soul also, which you have rescued.

Repeat Antiphon

Psalm Prayer

Lord God, you have always been my help. Even now, in the darkness of grief, when I cannot see you or feel you, I cry out to you. I remember your constant love, all the ways you have cared for me. And in the midst of my struggle, weak though my faith may be, I call you, my rock and my fortress. Hear my prayer, make haste to help me.

Reading

John 11:17–27 *Jesus reaches out to us, as he did to Martha, to draw us more closely to him.*

When Jesus arrived, he found that Lazarus had already been in the tomb four days. Now Bethany was near Jerusalem, some two miles away, and many of the Jews had come to Martha and Mary to console them about their brother. When Martha heard that Jesus was coming, she went and met him, while Mary stayed at home.

Martha said to Jesus, "Lord, if you had been here, my brother would not have died. But even now I know that God will give you whatever you ask of him." Jesus said to her, "Your brother will rise again."

Martha said to him, "I know that he will rise again in the resurrection on the last day." Jesus said to her, "I am the resurrection and the life. Those who believe in me, even though they die, will live, and everyone who lives and believes in me will never die. Do you believe this?" She said to him, "Yes, Lord, I believe that you are the Messiah, the Son of God, the one coming into the world."

Breath Prayer

Repeat this prayer in rhythm with your breathing for as long as you wish.

I believe Lord, but help my unbelief.

Closing Prayer

Pray the Our Father or one of the Canticles in the Everyday Prayer section of the book.

Abide With Me

Abide with me; fast falls the eventide;
the darkness deepens; Lord, with me abide!
When other helpers fail, and comforts flee,
help of the helpless, O abide with me.

Swift to its close ebbs out life's little day;
earth's joys grow dim, its glories pass away;
change and decay in all around I see;
O thou who changest not, abide with me.

Hold thou thy cross before my closing eyes;
shine through the gloom, and point me
   to the skies:
heaven's morning breaks, and earth's vain
   shadows flee;
in life, in death, O Lord, abide with me!
   —Henry Francis Lyte

Write Your Name On My Heart

Write your blessed name, O Lord, upon my heart,
there to remain so indelibly engraved,
that no prosperity, no adversity
shall ever move me from your love.
Be to me a strong tower of defense,
a comforter in tribulation, a deliverer in distress,
a very present help in trouble
and a guide to heaven
through the many temptations and dangers of
this life.
  —Thomas à Kempis

Like a Lost Child

Lord, I am like a lost child crying for its mother:
afraid to move, panicked, all alone.
Somehow it feels like it's my fault,
like I've run away, without ever wanting to.
Once you were near, easy to find,
your strong hand there to guide me,
your gentle voice close to comfort me.
What has happened to me?
How did I lose you? Or was it you who lost me?
Don't leave me here like this,
but come quickly to my rescue.
Put your arms around me and bring me back to you.

What Do I Know?

"Now I know there is a God," they say,
when death passes by, when prayers are
    answered.
So what do I know,
when death comes to stay,
when prayers are unheard?
That there is no God?
That death can't be staved off by prayer?
I don't have any easy answers to death's
    terrible questions.
All I know is that despite this pain,
    something remains;
that love is somehow not extinguished by death.

And I believe that this fierce love, this
    unquenchable longing
is not false, is not a cruel trick.
Rather I choose to trust that it is a compass
    within me
pointing me always into the heart of mystery,
pointing me always to home.

✑ Readings for Times of Weak Faith ✒

The Gap *Sometimes when we think that our faith is weak, the real problem is that we have not yet understood God's way of working in our lives.*

Nothing can make up for the absence of someone whom we love, and it would be wrong to try to find a substitute; we must simply hold out and see it through. That sounds very hard at first, but at the same time it is a great consolation, for the gap, as long as it remains unfilled, preserves the bonds between us. It is nonsense to say that God fills the gap; God doesn't fill it, but on the contrary, keeps it empty and so helps us to keep alive our former communion with each other, even at the cost of pain.
—Dietrich Bonhoeffer

1 Peter 1: 3–9 *Our faith is as precious as gold; and as gold is refined by fire, our faith can grow through suffering.*

Blessed be the God and Father of our Lord Jesus Christ! By his great mercy he has given us a new birth into a living hope through the resurrection of Jesus Christ from the dead, and into an inheritance that is imperishable, undefiled, and unfading, kept in heaven for you, who are being protected by the power of God through faith for a salvation ready to be revealed in the last time. In this you rejoice, even if now for a little while you have had to suffer various trials, so that the genuineness of your faith—being more precious than gold that, though perishable, is tested by fire—may be found to result in praise and glory and honor when Jesus Christ is revealed. Although you have not seen him, you love him; and even though you do not see him now, you believe in him and rejoice with an indescribable and glorious joy, for you are receiving the outcome of your faith, the salvation of your souls.

Chapter 6

When You Are Feeling Hopeless

Grieving is a long journey. Sometimes it seems like it will never end. Nothing we do and nothing anyone else can do—short of giving our beloved back to us—can make it better. We get tired, we feel empty, we lose hope.

It's so much easier to be hopeful when the end is in sight. But at the very heart of our struggle is not knowing what the future will be. Even if we believe, as St. Paul wrote, that "all things work together for the good," we still can't see that clearly. Real hope is not a comfortable clarity about the future. It is a dogged, sometimes even a desperate desire not to give in to the darkness. It is a cry of the heart for more, a refusal to give up or stop looking.

We can't conjure up hope out of nothing. Only God can give us hope. All we can do is ask for it and hold on as best we can.

❧ A Brief Time of Prayer ❧

Psalm 23

Antiphon: Though I walk through the darkest valley, you are with me.

The LORD is my shepherd, I shall not want.
He makes me lie down in green pastures;
he leads me beside still waters;
he restores my soul.
He leads me in right paths for his name's sake.
Even though I walk through the darkest valley,
I fear no evil;
for you are with me; your rod and your staff
they comfort me.
You prepare a table before me in the presence of
my enemies;
you anoint my head with oil; my cup overflows.
Surely goodness and mercy shall follow me
all the days of my life,
and I shall dwell in the house of the Lord
my whole life long.

Repeat Antiphon

Psalm Prayer

Help me, gentle Shepherd, for I am weak; the light of hope is fading from my eyes. Do not abandon me, for I trust in you. Like a lost and wounded sheep, I cry out to you. Lift me up, bind my wounds, carry me to safety. You alone are my hope.

Reading

John 11:32–45 *Jesus' love exceeds our expectation. As he taught Martha and Mary to trust in him, so too he teaches us.*

When Mary came where Jesus was and saw him, she knelt at his feet and said to him, "Lord, if you had been here, my brother would not have died." When Jesus saw her weeping, and the Jews who came with her also weeping, he was greatly disturbed in spirit and deeply moved. He said, "Where have you laid him?" They said to him, "Lord, come and see."

Jesus began to weep. So the Jews said, "See how he loved him!" But some of them said, "Could not he who opened the eyes of the blind man have kept this man from dying?"

Then Jesus, again greatly disturbed, came to the tomb. It was a cave, and a stone was lying against it. Jesus said, "Take away the stone." Martha, the sister of the dead man, said to him, "Lord, already there is a stench because he has been dead four days." Jesus said to her, "Did I not tell you that if you believed, you would see the glory of God?" So they took away the stone.

And Jesus looked upward and said, "Father, I thank you for having heard me. I knew that you always hear me, but I have said this for the sake of the crowd standing here, so that they may believe that you sent me." When he had said this, he cried with a loud voice, "Lazarus, come out!" The dead man came out, his hands and feet bound with strips of cloth, and his face wrapped in a cloth. Jesus said to them, "Unbind him, and let him go." Many of the Jews therefore, who had come with Mary and had seen what Jesus did, believed in him.

Breath Prayer

Repeat this prayer in rhythm with your breathing for as long as you wish.

You alone are my hope.

Closing Prayer

Pray the Our Father or one of the Canticles in the Everyday Prayers section of the book.

❧ Prayers for Times of Feeling Hopeless ❧

Choose Life

Blessed be your name, Lord God,
who has set before me life and death,
and has invited me to choose life.
Now, Lord God, I choose life, with all my heart.
I choose you, my God, for you are my life.
Lord, make me completely holy,
that all my spirit, soul and body
may be a temple for you.
Live in me, and be my God
and I will be your servant.
    —Thomas Ken

Come Softly, Spirit

Come softly, Spirit of God
into the hidden recesses of my heart
where hope has vanished and only
   emptiness remains.

Let the warmth of your breath revive me.
May the light of your fire renew me.
Through the power of your presence restore me.

Remind me of those who need me, who love me.
And give me the ability to hope that one day
I shall be united fully with you and my loved
ones in heaven.

Dependence On God's Mercy

Grant, Lord God, that in the middle of all
the discouragements,
difficulties and dangers, distress and darkness of
this mortal life,
I may depend on your mercy,
and build my hopes on this sure foundation.
Let your infinite mercy in Christ Jesus
deliver me from despair, both now and at the
hour of death.
—Thomas Wilson (alt.)

Christ, Our Hope

Pioneer on this journey, walk ever before me.
Pathfinder in the wilderness, let me not lose sight
of you.
Morning star in the gloom, rouse me
from discouragement.
True north in uncertainty, keep me on the
right road.
Anchor in the tumult, hold me fast to you.
Port in the storm, give me your protection.
Bridge across despair, be strong beneath me.
Gateway to life, bring me safely home.

❧ Readings for Times of Feeling Hopeless ❧

Ready to Help Us *In this quotation from the classic work* The Imitation of Christ, *Thomas à Kempis writes in the voice of Christ, who reminds us he is with us even in our moments of hopelessness.*

"I am more pleased to see patience and humility when things are difficult, than a state of devotion and spiritual joy when things go well. Whatever the trouble, put it out of your heart as best you can. Even if it does touch you, do not let it depress you, or keep you concerned for too long. If you cannot bear it joyfully, at least bear it patiently. I am still living," says the Lord, "and I am ready to help you and comfort you more than you have ever known, if you trust me and call on me."
    —Thomas à Kempis

Romans 8:31–39 *If we place ourselves in God's care, nothing can separate us from his love.*

What then are we to say about these things? If God is for us, who is against us? He who did not withhold his own Son, but gave him up for all of us, will he not with him also give us everything else? Who will bring any charge against God's elect? It is God who justifies. Who is to condemn? It is Christ Jesus, who died, yes, who was raised, who is at the right hand of God, who indeed intercedes for us. Who will separate us from the love of Christ? Will hardship, or distress, or persecution, or famine, or nakedness, or peril, or sword? As it is written, "For your sake we are being killed all day long; we are accounted as sheep to be slaughtered." No, in all these things we are more than conquerors through him who loved us. For I am convinced that neither death, nor life, nor angels, nor rulers, nor things present, nor things to come, nor powers, nor height, nor depth, nor anything else in all creation, will be able to separate us from the love of God in Christ Jesus our Lord.

Chapter 7

When You Want to Accept Your Loss

Accepting our loss doesn't mean we've gotten over it, that it's time to move on, or that the end of grieving is in sight. We know that after the death of a loved one, everything is different and there is no going back to the way it used to be. The loss will always hurt, and even the best of memories will be bittersweet.

We know all of this now. We've learned it the hard way. We don't want to accept it, but we know we have to. And at the same time we are allowing ourselves to open up gradually, to receive the goodness of life into our hearts. We see how much there is to live for, and we want to accept life with all its joys and pains. We are not there yet, but we can see it and we want to get there.

If we open our hearts in prayer, we can trust God's healing Spirit to lead us, each day, as far as we are able to go.

❧ A Brief Time of Prayer ❧

Psalm 57

Antiphon: Though my soul is weighed down, my heart is steadfast, O God.

Be merciful to me, O God, be merciful to me,
for in you my soul takes refuge;
in the shadow of your wings I will take refuge,
until the destroying storms pass by.

I cry to God Most High,
to God who fulfills his purpose for me.
He will send from heaven and save me,
he will put to shame those who trample on me.
God will send forth his steadfast love and
　　his faithfulness.

I lie down among lions that greedily devour
　　human prey;
their teeth are spears and arrows,
　　their tongues sharp swords.
Be exalted, O God, above the heavens.
Let your glory be over all the earth.

They set a net for my steps; my soul was
   bowed down.
They dug a pit in my path, but they have fallen
   into it themselves.
My heart is steadfast, O God, my heart is steadfast.
I will sing and make melody.

Awake, my soul! Awake, O harp and lyre!
I will awake the dawn.
I will give thanks to you, O Lord,
   among the peoples;
I will sing praises to you among the nations.

For your steadfast love is as high as the heavens;
your faithfulness extends to the clouds.
Be exalted, O God, above the heavens.
Let your glory be over all the earth.

Repeat Antiphon

Psalm Prayer

Have mercy on me, O God. Let the light of your
steadfast love dispel the darkness in my vacant
heart. My grief has emptied it of all emotion, now
only you can fill me. I long for your peace, your
comfort, your love. My heart is ready, O God, my
heart is ready.

Reading

Matthew 5:1–12 *In the Beatitudes, Jesus invites us to learn how our experience of loss can teach us how to care for others.*

When Jesus saw the crowds, he went up the mountain; and after he sat down, his disciples came to him. Then he began to speak, and taught them, saying:

"Blessed are the poor in spirit,
for theirs is the kingdom of heaven.

Blessed are those who mourn,
for they will be comforted.

Blessed are the meek,
for they will inherit the earth.

Blessed are those who hunger and thirst for righteousness,
for they will be filled.

Blessed are the merciful,
for they will receive mercy.

Blessed are the pure in heart,
for they will see God.

Blessed are the peacemakers,
for they will be called children of God.

Blessed are those who are persecuted for righteousness' sake,
for theirs is the kingdom of heaven.

Blessed are you when people revile you and
  persecute you
  and utter all kinds of evil against you falsely
  on my account.
Rejoice and be glad,
  for your reward is great in heaven. . . ."

Breath Prayer

*Repeat this prayer in rhythm with your breathing for
as long as you wish.*

Open my heart Lord, carefully, gently.

Closing Prayer

*Pray the Our Father or one of the Canticles in the
Everyday Prayers section of the book.*

❧ Prayers to Accept Your Loss ❧

You Are With Me

Lord, I know
whatever comfort I experience,
whatever hope I discover,
whatever peace I possess,
is a gift from you.
On my own
I could never accept this loss
or find the strength to go on.
But I recognize that within me
something stirs, a strength is emerging,
and I know it is not of my own making,
but is yours.
I know that you are with me,
and that with you,
all things are possible.

The Rainbow Through the Rain

O Joy that seekest me through pain,
I cannot close my heart to thee;
I trace the rainbow through the rain,
and feel the promise is not vain,
that morn shall tearless be.

  —George Matheson

Strong In You

Lord our God, we are in the shadow
  of your wings.
Protect us and bear us up.
You will care for us as if we were little children,
even to our old age.
When you are our strength, we are strong,
but when we are our own strength we are weak.
Our good always lives in your presence,
and we suffer when we turn our faces away from you.

We now return to you O Lord,
that we may never turn away again.

  —St. Augustine

O Risen Jesus

O risen Jesus, living one,
you embraced Mary in the garden,
and walked with your disciples on the road
   to Emmaus.
You urged Thomas to touch your wounds,
and cooked breakfast for your friends
   on the lakeshore.

Teach me to accept your comfort and strength
through the open embrace of my loved ones
who offer companionship as I walk this
   painful journey,
who are not afraid to touch my wounds,
who welcome me with the gift of their hospitality.

Together, O Lord, help us to recognize your presence,
as you continue to live among us.

❧ Readings for Times of Acceptance ❦

A Living Pietà *Accepting our loss is a way of cherishing all that has been.*

When Mary received the dead body of Jesus in her arms, she was taking back, receiving Jesus in his totality, with all the accompanying pain that came with holding his battered body. In that moment, Mary had come full circle with Jesus, receiving in death the bruised and beaten body of the son she had birthed as a fresh healthy child some thirty-three years earlier. Everything she had known and cherished about her son, all the love they had shared, the trials and tribulations they had experienced, each hope and dream she had for him, all this Mary held in her sorrowing lap.

The wounded Christ in Mary's lap is also in the lap of our lives. The Jesus of the *Pietà* is each suffering person who enters our life. We may be receiving the dead body of someone we love or we may be receiving a non-physical death (a great loss) that causes us, or someone else, immense grief. Being a living *Pietà* means that there are moments in life when we need to hold what has died, cherish what has been, and accept the reality of the pain that comes with this loss.

—Joyce Rupp

Revelation 21:1–7 *We find peace in knowing that the separation of death is not permanent.*

Then I saw a new heaven and a new earth; for the first heaven and the first earth had passed away, and the sea was no more. And I saw the holy city, the new Jerusalem, coming down out of heaven from God, prepared as a bride adorned for her husband. And I heard a loud voice from the throne saying, "See, the home of God is among mortals. He will dwell with them; they will be his peoples, and God himself will be with them; he will wipe every tear from their eyes. Death will be no more; mourning and crying and pain will be no more, for the first things have passed away."

And the one who was seated on the throne said, "See, I am making all things new." Also he said, "Write this, for these words are trustworthy and true." Then he said to me, "It is done! I am the Alpha and the Omega, the beginning and the end. To the thirsty I will give water as a gift from the spring of the water of life. Those who conquer will inherit these things, and I will be their God and they will be my children."

Chapter 8

When You Want to Pray for the Deceased

One of the prayers of the Funeral Mass reminds us that in death "life is changed, not ended."

The lives of our deceased loved ones go on. They are with God, and although we cannot see or hear them, we believe that they are still with us. And because we believe that the resurrection of Jesus has overcome the power of death, we believe that through Christ the bond of love we shared remains alive, strong, and personal.

We pray for our loved ones not only so that they may live eternally in God's presence, but also to remember and to strengthen the bond we share with them. We pray for them, just as they pray for us, so that one day we may be fully united, in a new and deeper way than ever before. We ask them to join us in prayer for our shared concerns, and we may ask them to pray especially for certain people. We pray *for* our loved ones; and we pray *with* our loved ones. And we do this for the simple reason that we love each other and we love our God who sustains us still.

❧ A Brief Time of Prayer ❦

Psalm 103:1–18

Antiphon: In life and in death, we are yours,
O Lord.

Bless the LORD, O my soul,
and all that is within me, bless his holy name.
Bless the LORD, O my soul,
and do not forget all his benefits—
who forgives all your iniquity,
who heals all your diseases,
who redeems your life from the Pit,
who crowns you with steadfast love and mercy,
who satisfies you with good as long as you live
so that your youth is renewed like the eagle's.
The LORD works vindication
and justice for all who are oppressed.
He made known his ways to Moses,
his acts to the people of Israel.
The LORD is merciful and gracious,
slow to anger and abounding in steadfast love.
He will not always accuse,
nor will he keep his anger forever.
He does not deal with us according to our sins,

nor repay us according to our iniquities.
For as the heavens are high above the earth,
so great is his steadfast love toward those who
    fear him;
as far as the east is from the west,
so far he removes our transgressions from us.

As a father has compassion for his children,
so the LORD has compassion for those who
    fear him.
For he knows how we were made;
he remembers that we are dust.
As for mortals, their days are like grass;
they flourish like a flower of the field;
for the wind passes over it, and it is gone,
and its place knows it no more.

But the steadfast love of the LORD
is from everlasting to everlasting on those
    who fear him,
and his righteousness to children's children,
to those who keep his covenant
and remember to do his commandments.

Repeat Antiphon

Psalm Prayer

Merciful God, the death of your Son broke the bonds of death, and opened for us the unending path of life. Your care is with us all of our lives, and in death, you fill us with your presence. I place my beloved who has died in your care, O Lord, and rely on your strength to sustain me on this journey.

Reading

Wisdom 3:1–9 *We entrust our loved one to God, confident in his grace and mercy.*

But the souls of the righteous are in the hand of God, and no torment will ever touch them. In the eyes of the foolish they seemed to have died, and their departure was thought to be a disaster, and their going from us to be their destruction; but they are at peace. For though in the sight of others they were punished, their hope is full of immortality. Having been disciplined a little, they will receive great good, because God tested them and found them worthy of himself; like gold in the furnace he tried them, and like a sacrificial burnt offering he accepted them. In the time of their visitation they will shine forth, and will run like sparks through the stubble. They will govern nations and rule over peoples, and the Lord will reign over them forever.

Those who trust in him will understand truth, and the faithful will abide with him in love, because grace and mercy are upon his holy ones, and he watches over his elect.

Breath Prayer

Repeat this prayer in rhythm with your breathing for as long as you wish.

Our lives are in your hands, O Lord.

Closing Prayer

Pray the Our Father or one of the Canticles in the Everyday Prayers section of the book.

❧ Prayers for Our Loved Ones ❧

Receive This Soul

Saints of God, come to his/her aid!
Hasten to meet him/her, angels of the Lord!
Receive his/her soul and present him/her to God
the Most High.

May Christ who called you take you to himself;
may angels lead you to the bosom of Abraham.
Receive his/her soul and present him/her to God
the Most High.

Eternal rest grant unto him/her O Lord,
and let perpetual light shine upon him/her.
Receive his/her soul and present him/her to God
the Most High.
    —The Rite of Funerals

For the Faithful Departed

By the merits of your rising from the dead,
Lord Christ,
let death no longer have dominion
over the faithful departed.
Grant to your servants
a resting place in your eternal mansions
and in the arms of Abraham and Sarah,
our ancestors in the faith.
Grant this to all who,
from Adam and Eve to this day,
have served you with a clean heart—
to our mothers and fathers,
to our sisters and brothers,
to our friends and kindred.
Make a place in your heavenly kingdom, Lord,
for everyone who has done you faithful service
in this present life
and to all who, in their fashion,
have striven toward you.

   —An Ancient Prayer

For Eternal Rest

O God, the Creator and Redeemer of all the faithful, grant to the souls of your servants departed full remission of their sins, that, through our devout prayers, they may obtain pardon, which they have always desired. Who live and reign, world without end. Amen.

Eternal rest grant unto them, O Lord.
And let perpetual light shine upon them.
May he/she rest in peace.
Amen.

May his/her soul, and all the souls of the faithful departed,
through the mercy of God, rest in peace. Amen.
— Traditional

Life's Tempestuous Sea

Blessed are all your saints, our God and King,
who have traveled over life's tempestuous sea,
and have arrived in the harbor of peace
    and felicity.
Watch over us who are still in our
    dangerous voyage;
and remember those who lie exposed
to the rough storms of trouble and temptations.

Frail is our vessel, and the ocean is wide;
but as in your mercy you have set our course,
so steer the vessel of our life toward the
    everlasting shore of peace,
and bring us at length to the quiet haven of our
    heart's desire,
where you, O our God, are blessed,
and live and reign for ever and ever.
    —St. Augustine

❧ Readings About Prayer for the Deceased ❦

The Risen Christ, Our Hope *Though we are pained by our separation, we pray to one day be reunited in Christ.*

"Lazarus our friend is sleeping." In saying this, Christ who is the hope of all believers refers to the departed as those who are asleep. By no means does he regard them as dead.

Paul the apostle does not want us to grieve about those who have fallen asleep. Our faith tells us that all who believe in Christ will never die; indeed faith assures us that Christ is not dead, nor shall we die.

The Lord himself will come down from Heaven and there will be the command of the archangel's voice and the sound of the trumpet; then those who are united with Christ in death will rise.

Let the hope of the resurrection encourage us, then, because we shall see again those whom we lose here below. Of course we must continue to believe firmly in Christ; we must continue to obey his commandments. His power is so great that it is easier for him to raise the dead to life than it is for us to arouse those who are sleeping. . . .

O death! You separate those who are joined to each other in marriage. You harshly and cruelly divide those whom friendship unites. But your power is broken. . . . And with the words of the Apostle [Paul] we, too, deride you, " O death! Where is your victory? O death! Where is your sting?"

—From a letter by St. Braulio

Ephesians 6:18 *We pray for those whom we love, living or deceased, simply because we love them.*

Pray in the Spirit at all times in every prayer and supplication. To that end keep alert and always persevere in supplication for all the saints.

Chapter 9

When You Are Grateful

Gratitude is a sign of healing. Even in the midst of our sorrow, we are beginning to see beyond it. When we can acknowledge the ways God has blessed us through our loved one, or when we can recognize God's grace at work in our lives, it is a sign that we are moving ahead on our journey, from the natural and necessary focus on our pain and loss to a new and wider vantage point from which we can see beyond ourselves and our hurts.

To be grateful is to remember. But remembering can be painful. At first when we remember, we may naturally ask, "Why is he or she gone?" or "How could this happen?" But when, alongside those questions, the response of gratitude and appreciation surfaces, we are on our way to a new kind of wholeness. We are beginning to grow strong in the broken places.

❧ A Brief Time of Prayer ❧

Psalm 92:1–8, 12–15

Antiphon: I give you thanks, O Lord, for your steadfast love and faithfulness.

It is good to give thanks to the LORD,
to sing praises to your name, O Most High;
to declare your steadfast love in the morning,
and your faithfulness by night,
to the music of the lute and the harp,
to the melody of the lyre.

For you, O LORD, have made me glad
   by your work;
at the works of your hands I sing for joy.
How great are your works, O LORD!
Your thoughts are very deep!

The dullard cannot know,
the stupid cannot understand this:
though the wicked sprout like grass and all
   evildoers flourish,
they are doomed to destruction forever,
but you, O LORD, are on high forever.

The righteous flourish like the palm tree,
and grow like a cedar in Lebanon.
They are planted in the house of the LORD;
they flourish in the courts of our God.

In old age they still produce fruit;
they are always green and full of sap,
showing that the LORD is upright; he is my rock,
and there is no unrighteousness in him.

Repeat Antiphon

Psalm Prayer

It is good to give you thanks, O Lord, for the
many ways your love has sustained me in this
time of grief. In sadness, in loneliness, in pain,
and in confusion, you have been with me. Thank
you for the comfort of your presence and for the
light of faith that continues to guide me through
the difficult passage. You are my hope.

Reading

John 6:51–59 *In the Eucharist, our greatest prayer of thanksgiving, we are united with Jesus and all those who ate this Living Bread.*

"I am the living bread that came down from heaven. Whoever eats of this bread will live forever; and the bread that I will give for the life of the world is my flesh."

The Jews then disputed among themselves, saying, "How can this man give us his flesh to eat?" So Jesus said to them, "Very truly, I tell you, unless you eat the flesh of the Son of Man and drink his blood, you have no life in you. Those who eat my flesh and drink my blood have eternal life, and I will raise them up on the last day; for my flesh is true food and my blood is true drink. Those who eat my flesh and drink my blood abide in me, and I in them. Just as the living Father sent me, and I live because of the Father, so whoever eats me will live because of me. This is the bread that came down from heaven, not like that which your ancestors ate, and they died. But the one who eats this bread will live forever." He said these things while he was teaching in the synagogue at Capernaum.

Breath Prayer

Repeat this prayer in rhythm with your breathing for as long as you wish.

Abide in me.

Closing Prayer

Pray the Our Father or one of the Canticles in the Everyday Prayers section of the book.

❧ Prayers of Gratitude ☙

For Faith, Hope, and Love

Gracious God, giver of all good gifts
thank you for the gift of (*name*),
and for the many gifts you gave him/her
to live a Christian life.

Thank you for (*name's*) gift of faith:
for the ways he/she was able to see life
   as a journey
with you as both companion and guide,
and for the gift of perseverance even in doubt
or confusion.

Thank you for (*name's*) gift of hope:
for the ways he/she joyfully embraced life,
encouraged others who were down,
and found the light amid the darkness.

And most of all thank you for (*name's*) gift of love:
for his/her generosity and thoughtfulness,
patience and kindness,
self-sacrifice and forgiveness.

Through these gifts we too have been strengthened
in faith, hope, and love.
Help us to persevere on our journey to you
so that we may one day see you and (name) face
to face.

Deo Gratias

Thanks be to God for his goodness to me.
Thanks be to God now and in eternity.
Thanks be to God for the wonders he has done.
Thanks be to God for his dear and only son.
Thanks be to God for our sweet virgin mother.
Thanks be to God for becoming our brother.
Thanks be to God for his body and his blood.
Thanks be to God for his legacy of love.
Thanks be to God for his sacred heart benign.
Thanks be to God for this treasure divine.
Thanks be to God for my angel guardian bright.
Thanks be to God for morning, noon, and night.
Thanks be to God in all ages and all climes.
Thanks be to God one hundred thousand times.
Thanks be to God in my joy and in my sorrow.
Thanks be to God for today and for tomorrow.
Thanks be to God in my illness and my health.
Thanks be to God both in poverty and wealth.
Thanks be to God at my work and at my prayers.
Thanks be to God in my troubles and in my cares.
Thanks be to God in my life and at my death.
Thanks be to God when drawing my last breath.

And when, lifeless, my poor heart shall lie
   under the sod,
May my soul sing in heaven,
Thanks be to Thee, O good and generous God.
   —Author unknown

Come, My Way

Come, my Way, my Truth, my Life:
Such a Way as gives us breath:
Such a Truth as ends of strife:
Such a Life as killeth death.

Come, my Light, my Feast, my Strength:
Such a Light, as shows a feast:
Such a Feast, as mends in length:
Such a Strength, as makes his guest.

Come, my Joy, my Love, my Heart:
Such a Joy, as none can move:
Such a Love, as none can part:
Such a Heart, as joys in love.
   —George Herbert

Celebrate Life and Death *Losing a loved one reminds us of the intimate connection between life and death and of how precious life is. This awareness is what enables us to be grateful.*

When we speak about celebration we tend to bring to mind happy, pleasant, gay festivities in which we can forget for a while the hardships of life and immerse ourselves in an atmosphere of music, dance, drinks, laughter and a lot of cozy small-talk. But celebration in the Christian sense has very little to do with this. Celebration is only possible through the deep realization that life and death are never found completely separate. Celebration can really completely come about only where fear and love, joy and sorrow, tears and smiles can exist together. Celebration is the acceptance of life in a constantly increasing awareness of preciousness. And life is precious not only because it can be seen, touched, and tasted, but also because it will be gone one day.

When we have been able to celebrate life in all [its] decisive moments where gaining and losing, that is life and death, touched each other all the time, we will be able to celebrate even our own dying because we have learned from life that he who loses it can find it (Matthew 16:25).

—Henri Nouwen

Isaiah 25:6–9 *We remember with gratitude the many joyful celebrations we shared with our loved one, and we look forward to the heavenly banquet.*

On this mountain the LORD of hosts will make for all peoples a feast of rich food, a feast of well-aged wines, of rich food filled with marrow, of well-aged wines strained clear. And he will destroy on this mountain the shroud that is cast over all peoples, the sheet that is spread over all nations; he will swallow up death forever. Then the Lord GOD will wipe away the tears from all faces, and the disgrace of his people he will take away from all the earth, for the LORD has spoken. It will be said on that day, Lo, this is our God; we have waited for him, so that he might save us. This is the LORD for whom we have waited; let us be glad and rejoice in his salvation.

Chapter 10

When You Want to Remember

We never want to forget those we love deeply. We want to remember everything about them, all the little things we loved so much. We want to remember our relationship, the love we shared, the difference this person made in our lives. And we want others to remember as well, to acknowledge and honor the one we loved. Even though it is painful at first, we cling to those memories. We cherish special things; we mark important days. We tell stories, repeat old sayings, revisit important places.

Prayer is the most important way of remembering. When we pray we tap into a power that is greater than our power of recollection, a power that endures beyond photos or keepsakes. When we pray we place ourselves in the presence of our eternal and loving God, whose hands hold both the living and the dead, and whose promise that we will one day be reunited is trustworthy.

❧ A Brief Time of Prayer ❧

Psalm 63:1–8

Antiphon: Your love is better than life.

O God, you are my God, I seek you,
my soul thirsts for you; my flesh faints for you,
as in a dry and weary land where there is no water.
So I have looked upon you in the sanctuary,
beholding your power and glory.

Because your steadfast love is better than life,
my lips will praise you.
So I will bless you as long as I live;
I will lift up my hands and call on your name.

My soul is satisfied as with a rich feast,
and my mouth praises you with joyful lips
when I think of you on my bed,
and meditate on you in the watches of the night;

for you have been my help,
and in the shadow of your wings I sing for joy.
My soul clings to you;
your right hand upholds me.

Repeat Antiphon

Psalm Prayer

Let me never forget, O Lord, the many ways you have graced me with the love of (*name of your loved one*). The love we shared is a reflection of your love, and even the memory of it sustains me. Make us one in you, for you have always been our help.

Reading

Matthew 25:31–40 *Imagine your loved one standing before the Lord, engaged in this conversation.*

"When the Son of Man comes in his glory, and all the angels with him, then he will sit on the throne of his glory. All the nations will be gathered before him, and he will separate people one from another as a shepherd separates the sheep from the goats, and he will put the sheep at his right hand and the goats at the left.

"Then the king will say to those at his right hand, 'Come, you that are blessed by my Father, inherit the kingdom prepared for you from the foundation of the world; for I was hungry and you gave me food, I was thirsty and you gave me something to drink, I was a stranger and you welcomed me, I was naked and you gave me clothing, I was sick and you took care of me, I was in prison and you visited me.'

"Then the righteous will answer him, 'Lord, when was it that we saw you hungry and gave you food, or thirsty and gave you something to drink? And when was it that we saw you a stranger and welcomed you, or naked and gave you clothing? And when was it that we saw you sick or in prison and visited you?'

"And the king will answer them, 'Truly I tell you, just as you did it to one of the least of these who are members of my family, you did it to me.'"

Breath Prayer

Repeat this prayer in rhythm with your breathing for as long as you wish.

"Love one another, as I have loved you."

Closing Prayer

Pray the Our Father or one of the Canticles in the Everyday Prayers section of the book.

❧ Prayers of Remembrance for Our Loved Ones ❧

Our Pilgrimage

O Lord God, from whom we come,
In whom we are enfolded, to whom we shall return:
Bring us in our pilgrimage through life;
  With the power of the Father protecting,
  With the love of Jesus indwelling,
  And the light of the Spirit guiding,
Until we come to our ending,
In life and love eternal.
  —Peter Nott

When I Was Hungry

When I was hungry, it was you, Lord, who fed me through the nurture of (*your loved one's name*).

When I was thirsty, you refreshed me through the kindness of (*name*).

When I was lonely, you were my companion through the friendship of (*name*).

When I was sad, you comforted me through the compassion of (*name*).

When I was searching, you guided me through the understanding of (*name*).

When I rejoiced, you celebrated with me in the joyfulness of (*name*).

Now, Lord, I am grieving and it is painful to remember. Help me to realize that in every moment we shared, you were with us. It was your love we experienced, your Spirit that united us. As I remember these moments, may the sadness of loss be lightened by the recognition of your care. And may your Spirit continue to unite us, not only in memory, but in the hope of the resurrection.

In Memory of . . .

On the night before you died, Lord,
you took bread and broke it,
you took wine and poured it,
you fed your friends with your very self.
Then you took a basin and towel
and washed their feet.
And you said, "Do this in memory of me."

As you called us to remember you
not just in word but in action,
help me to remember (*name*)
not only by recalling words of your loved one
but by living the legacy of his/her gifts.

Teach me, Lord, to break anew the bread of
 his/her goodness,
to pour out for others the wine of
 his/her kindness,
to humbly serve others as he/she served us.
In some way, Lord,
may my life be a testament
to the gifts you gave (*name*).
Teach me to live in memory of him/her,
as he/she lived in memory of you.

❧ Readings for Times of Remembering ❧

You All Along *As we remember our loved ones who have died, we are remembering the many ways God touched us through them.*

So it was you all along. Everyone I ever loved, it was you. Everything decent or fine that ever happened to me, everything that ever made me reach out and try to be better, it was you all along.
—C. S. Lewis

1 Corinthians 13:1–8 *We remember all the ways we have been graced by the gift of love from our deceased loved one.*

If I speak in the tongues of mortals and of angels, but do not have love, I am a noisy gong or a clanging cymbal. And if I have prophetic powers, and understand all mysteries and all knowledge, and if I have all faith, so as to remove mountains, but do not have love, I am nothing. If I give away all my possessions, and if I hand over my body so that I may boast, but do not have love, I gain nothing. Love is patient; love is kind; love is not envious or boastful or arrogant or rude. It does not insist on its own way; it is not irritable or resentful; it does not rejoice in wrongdoing, but rejoices in the truth. It bears all things, believes all things, hopes all things, endures all things. Love never ends.

Index of Prayers

Abide With Me / Henry Francis Lyte ... 63

Be Within Me Lord / Lancelot Andrewes ... 46

Canticle of Mary ... 17
Canticle of Simeon ... 19
Canticle of Zachary ... 15
Choose Life / Thomas Ken ... 72
Christ, Our Hope / author ... 74
Come Softly, Spirit / author ... 72
Come, My Way / George Herbert ... 107

Deo Gratias / author unknown ... 105
Dependence On God's Mercy / Thomas Wilson ... 73

Evening Prayer / St. Columba ... 14
Experiencing Loss / Joyce Rupp ... 24

For Eternal Rest / traditional ... 94
For Faith, Hope, and Love / author ... 103
For Strength In Weakness / author unknown ... 53
For the Faithful Departed / an ancient prayer ... 93

I Am Afraid / author ... 44
I Heard the Voice of Jesus Say / Horatius Bonar ... 55
In Memory of . . . / author ... 116

Just Be Here, Lord / author ... 34

Lead, Kindly Light / John Henri Newman ... 45
Life's Tempestuous Sea / St. Augustine ... 95
Like a Lost Child / author ... 64

Morning Prayer / St. Francis de Sales ... 13

Night Prayer / Roman Breviary ... 14

O Good Shepherd / author ... 54
O Living God / William Bridge ... 27
O Risen Jesus / author ... 84
Our Pilgrimage / Peter Nott ... 114

The Rainbow Through the Rain / George Matheson ... 83
Receive This Soul / The Rite of Funerals ... 92

Stabat Mater / Jacopone da Todi ... 26
Strong In You / St. Augustine ... 83

The Torn Curtain / author ... 25

Weak and Weary / author ... 54
Were You Angry Too, Jesus? / author ... 35
What Do I Know? / author ... 65
When Anger Imprisons You / Mary, Queen of Scots ... 36
When I Was Hungry / author ... 115
Why God? / author ... 36
Write Your Name On My Heart / Thomas à Kempis ... 64

You Are With Me / author ... 82

Acknowledgments

Unattributed works are by the author. A brief description of lesser known writers, whose prayers are in the public domain, is provided.

Readings

"Acknowledge Your Pain" by Ann Dawson is excerpted from *A Season of Grief*, Notre Dame, IN: Ave Maria Press, 2002. Used by permission.

"Anger Is Often Difficult" by Jean-Pierre de Caussade is excerpted from *Abandonment to Divine Providence*, New York: Doubleday & Co., 1975. De Caussade was an eighteenth-century French Jesuit.

"Celebrate Life and Death" by Henri Nouwen is excerpted from *Creative Ministry*, Garden City, NY: Doubleday, 1971, pp. 91–92.

"The Gap" by Dietrich Bonhoeffer is quoted from *God Knows You're Grieving* by Joan Guntzelman, Notre Dame, IN: Sorin Books, 2001. Bonhoeffer was a Lutheran pastor executed by the Nazis.

"A Living *Pietà*" by Joyce Rupp is excerpted from *Your Sorrow Is My Sorrow*, New York: Crossroad Publishing, 1999.

"Patient Endurance" is excerpted from *The Committed Life: An Adaptation of the Introduction to the Devout Life by St. Francis de Sales*, by William A. Meninger, New York: Continuum, 2000.

"Putting Fear Into Perspective" by Doug Hill is excerpted from *The Power of Prayerful Living*, Emmaus, PA: Rodale Books, 2001.

"Ready to Help Us," by Thomas à Kempis is excerpted from *The Imitation of Christ*, translated by Betty I. Knott, HarperCollins Publishers, Ltd., 1990, Book 3, LVII, 178.

"The Risen Christ, Our Hope" from a letter by St. Braulio is excerpted from *The Liturgy of the Hours, Volume IV*, New York: Catholic Book Publishing Company, 1975, pp. 1902–1903. St. Braulio was Bishop of Saragossa in Spain in the seventh century.

Prayers

"Abide With Me" is by Henry Francis Lyte, an English clergyman and composer of hymns in the nineteenth century.

"Be Within Me Lord" is by Lancelot Andrewes (1555–1626), Bishop of Winchester in England.

"Choose Life" is by Thomas Ken (1637–1711), who composed many prayers during his lifetime and was Bishop of Bath and Wells in England.

"Come, My Way" is by George Herbert (1593–1633), a poet and Anglican minister.

"Deo Gratias" is from *A Maryknoll Book of Prayer*, edited by Michael Leach and Susan Perry, Maryknoll, NY: Orbis Books, 2003, p. 278. Used by permission. Although the author is unknown, the prayer was submitted by Robert P. Hopkins of Ardsley, Pennsylvania, a friend of Maryknoll who learned it from a 108-year-old woman he visited as a eucharistic minister. She said it from memory.

"Dependence on God's Mercy" is by Thomas Wilson (1524–1581), an English philosopher and writer.

"Experiencing Loss" by Joyce Rupp is from *Your Sorrow Is My Sorrow* copyright © 1999 Joyce Rupp. Used by permission of The Crossroad Publishing Company, New York, NY.

"I Heard the Voice of Jesus Say" is by Horatius Bonar, a nineteenth-century Presbyterian minister and composer in Scotland.

"Lead, Kindly Light" is by John Henri Newman (1801–1890), a convert to Catholicism, a theologian, and a cardinal.

"O Living God" is by William Bridge, a seventeenth-century Puritan pastor in London.

"Our Pilgrimage" is by Peter Nott, the bishop of Norwich, England.

"The Rainbow Through the Rain" is by George Matheson (1842–1906), a minister in the Church of Scotland who suffered from very poor vision.

"*Stabat Mater*" by Jacopone da Todi, trans. by Anthony G. Petti, © 1971 Faber Music Ltd. Reproduced from *New Catholic Hymnal* by kind permission of the publisher.

"When Anger Imprisons You" is by Mary, Queen of Scots, who exhibited extraordinary perseverance and faith during the time of the Reformation in Great Britain.

"Write Your Name on My Heart" is by Thomas à Kempis, a fifteenth-century German priest.

ROBERT M. HAMMA, Editorial Director at Ave Maria Press, Inc., is the author of nine books and numerous articles on spirituality and family life, including *Earth's Echo: Sacred Encounters with Nature*. He holds an MA in theology from the University of Notre Dame as well as an MDiv from Immaculate Conception Seminary in Huntington, New York. Formerly an editor at Paulist Press, Hamma has also done hospital chaplaincy and parish ministry. He lives with his wife Kathryn Schneider and their three children in Granger, Indiana.